Frederick Phisterer

The Regular Brigade of the Fourteenth Army Corps,

the Army of the Cumberland, in the battle of Stone River, or

Murfreesboro', Tennessee, from December 31st, 1862, to January 3d,

1863

Frederick Phisterer

The Regular Brigade of the Fourteenth Army Corps,
the Army of the Cumberland, in the battle of Stone River, or Murfreesboro',
Tennessee, from December 31st, 1862, to January 3d, 1863

ISBN/EAN: 9783337301323

Printed in Europe, USA, Canada, Australia, Japan

Cover: Foto ©ninafisch / pixelio.de

More available books at **www.hansebooks.com**

THE

REGULAR BRIGADE

OF

THE FOURTEENTH ARMY CORPS,

THE ARMY OF THE CUMBERLAND,

IN THE BATTLE OF

STONE RIVER, OR MURFREESBORO', TENNESSEE,

FROM DECEMBER 31ST, 1862, TO JANUARY 3D, 1863,

BOTH DATES INCLUSIVE.

BY

FREDERICK PHISTERER,

Late Adjutant 2d Battalion 18th U. S. Infantry.

To his Comrades,

THE SURVIVORS OF THE REGULAR BRIGADE,

ARMY OF THE CUMBERLAND,

IN REMEMBRANCE OF PAST DAYS,

AND TO PLACE ON RECORD A TRUE ACCOUNT

OF THE

PARTICIPATION OF THE BRIGADE

IN THE

BATTLE OF STONE RIVER.

JULY 1ST, 1883.

WHEN General Rosecrans took command of the Army of the Ohio there were in that army five battalions of regular infantry in two different divisions; when he reorganized this army he determined to bring these battalions together, to give them a regular battery, and form of them a Regular Brigade. The 15th, 16th and 19th were already at Nashville; the orders organizing the brigade found the two battalions of the 18th near Gallatin, Tenn., as a part of General Stedman's Brigade. On receipt of the orders, the 18th marched, on the 23d of December, 1862, from Pilot Knob to Nashville, Tenn., arriving there on the 25th day of December, 1862, and, joining the other battalions and the battery, it completed the formation of the brigade, which, as then organized, consisted of:

The 1st Battalion of the 15th Infantry: Companies A, B, C, D, E, F, G and H; commanded by Major John H. King.

The 1st Battalion of the 16th Infantry: Companies A, B, C, D, E, F, G and H, 1st Battalion, and Company B, 2d Battalion; Major A. J. Slemmer commanding.

The 1st Battalion of the 18th Infantry: Companies A, B, C, D, E, F, G and H, of the 1st, and A and D, of the 3d Battalion; Major J. N. Caldwell in command.

The 2d Battalion of the 18th Infantry : Companies A, B, C, D, E and F, of the 2d, and B, C, E and F, of the 3d Battalion ; commanded by Major Frederick Townsend.

The 1st Battalion of the 19th Infantry : Companies A, B, C, D, E and F ; Major S. D. Carpenter commanding.

Battery H, 5th U. S. Artillery, commanded by 1st Lieutenant F. L. Guenther.

Lieutenant-Colonel O. L. Shepherd, 18th U. S. Infantry, the senior officer, was placed in command of the brigade.

When the Army of the Ohio—then become the Army of the Cumberland, or the 14th Corps—advanced from Nashville, Tenn., toward its objective point, the enemy, the Regular Brigade broke camp on the 26th, encamping on the evening of that day on the Petersburg Turnpike ; on the 27th it encamped near Nolansville, Tenn.; on the 28th, at night, it marched across the country to Stewart's Creek, and on the 30th to a point on the Murfreesboro' and Nashville Turnpike about four miles from Murfreesboro', Tenn.

On the morning of the 31st of December the brigade left its bivouac at an early hour and advanced on the Nashville Turnpike to a point a little less than three miles northwest of Murfreesboro', and, with its division, was posted in reserve. The division consisted of Scribner's, John Beatty's, Starkweather's and the Regular Brigade, and was commanded by Major-General Lovell H. Rousseau. Starkweather's Brigade had been left at Jefferson's Crossing on Stone River. The division was part of the centre, commanded by Major-General George H. Thomas. The formation in the brigade was from right to left as follows : 15th, 16th, 18th, 1st and 2d Battalions, and the 19th.

To fully understand the events now following, it will be necessary to preface them with a short résumé of the opening and progress of the battle from 6.30 A. M. until noon; from the right of the army to the left of Palmer's Division of the left wing.

The left of Palmer's Division, Hazen's Brigade, rested on the Nashville Turnpike, about two and a half miles northwest of Murfreesboro', facing south by east—the other brigades of this division faced almost east ; Negley's Division, of the centre, next in order, faced south by east ; Sheridan's, of the right wing, faced almost east ; Davis' faced south by east, and Johnson's, the right of the army, east and south, and a portion of it on the right flank west by south. A line drawn from the extreme right due north would have crossed the Nashville Turnpike near General Rosecrans' headquarters, about one mile northwest of Hazen.

All the divisions, excepting Palmer's and the left of Negley's, had to cross a dense cedar forest about three-quarters of a mile deep before they could reach the Nashville Turnpike to their left and rear.

The extreme right of Johnson's Division was attacked about 6.30 A. M., and the engagement extended gradually toward our left, the attacking columns of the enemy moving in echelon from their left to their right; the attack struck Johnson's flank, and, although portions of the division made a gallant stand, the weight of the attack was too much for the division. Johnson having been flanked and driven back, it became Davis' turn to be taken in rear and right flank, and forced back after considerable resistance. The next division, Sheridan's, was forewarned, and offered a most determined resistance, falling back and changing front to the west as its flank and rear became vulnerable; ammunition falling short, the rebel force on his flank increasing, Sheridan commenced his retreat about 9.30 A. M., falling back slowly and fighting. Negley necessarily had now to refuse his right, change front to the west and northwest, and, running out of ammunition about 11 A. M., commence his retreat out of the cedars. This exposed the right of Palmer's Division, compelling him, after a sharp fight, to change front to the west and fall back on the railroad, pivoting his division on the left of Hazen's Brigade, until it was at right angles with its former position; this took place about noon.

The general front of the line, which in the
morning was south by east, was now west by
south; the new line formed about noon ran
along the railroad and turnpike, and in front of it
were open fields from Hazen's left to a point
about one-eighth of a mile southeast of General
Rosecrans' headquarters, from which point the
now re-organized right wing was posted in the
forest in a semicircle facing south and west, with
the right, refused, facing north by west and rest-
ing near the turnpike. Between the right wing
and Palmer's Division there were Van Cleeve's
Division of the left wing, the Pioneer Brigade,
Negley's and Rousseau's Divisions.

During the remainder of the day these positions were not materially changed, except that
Van Cleeve's and Negley's Divisions were later
withdrawn and placed in reserve.

To return to the Regular Brigade : About 9
o'clock A. M. it became apparent that the tide of
battle was most decidedly against the right wing
of the army, and Rousseau's Division was ordered
to the support of General McCook. The Regular
Brigade with its battery moved by the right flank
into the dense wood of cedars, alluded to above ;
when near Sheridan the head of the brigade
changed direction to the right, and line of battle
was formed in the cedars facing west. Meanwhile it had become evident that on this ground
no use could be made of the battery, and that no

good position could be obtained for the infantry ; the advance was therefore discontinued and the battery with the brigade ordered by General Rousseau to the open field between the cedars and the turnpike, near where it started from.

Guenther's Battery first took position on a slight rise outside of the woods, but moved shortly to a knoll between the turnpike and railroad, shelling the woods in the direction of the advance of the enemy. The two right battalions, the 15th and 16th, not receiving the orders to halt, continued their advance, deployed skirmishers, and soon became engaged with a rebel force sweeping down in the rear of Sheridan. This force appeared to be clothed in the Union Blue, and for a time there was an uncertainty as to its character ; the skirmishers being soon driven in, the status of these troops was quickly developed and the battalions had a hot and fierce fight for a short time, in which they were assisted by the 6th Ohio Volunteer Regiment on their right. Majors King and Slemmer having finally received information of the movement of the brigade, prepared to rejoin it, falling back through the woods, and halting twice to repulse the enemy. Other forces coming to the support of the right, and Sheridan having changed front and refused his right, enabled these battalions to rejoin the brigade. Among the killed in this affair was Captain Bell, of the 15th. The other battalions,

though under fire, did not come into action, but
covered the movements, and followed in support
of their battery, all taking, finally, position on a
rise or knoll near the turnpike. At this point
the 19th was shifted from the left to the right
wing between the 15th and 16th, thereby equal-
izing the strength of the two wings more nearly.
While in this position, the line facing southwest,
the brigade, the battalions of the 18th, and the
battery especially, were exposed to an enfilading
artillery fire, and Captain Denison, of the 2d
Battalion, was mortally wounded, and Sergeant
White, of Co. F. 3d Battalion, 18th infantry, was
killed by a solid shot. The brigade was not long
in position when Sheridan's troops began to come
out of the woods, followed shortly after by the
enemy, whose further advance was resisted by it.
At a point where a short thicket about half way
between the battery and the woods and nearly
opposite the battery and right of the brigade
covered to some extent its approach, Wither's
Division formed and made a desperate charge on
Guenther's Battery. The enemy advanced boldly
and bravely; Guenther turned his admirably
served guns on him, and with the fire of his sup-
ports broke the column, which made four gallant
efforts to continue the charge, but melted away
under the dreadful fire; their battle flag went
down three times in succession. Portions of
Scribner's Brigade flanked the enemy's left, and,

upon the repulse of his charge on the Regular
Battery, Scribner's and John Beatty's Brigades,
Van Cleeve's Division, the Pioneer Brigade and
other organizations, led by Generals Rosecrans
and Rousseau in turn, charged upon the enemy,
driving him well back into the cedars. The
remnants of the right wing having meanwhile
been reorganized, reformed nearly all on the
right, advanced and took positions, held by them
until the close of the battle. The enemy's advance on our right and his flanking operations
had now been successfully resisted, but Negley
was still in the woods, flanked and almost sur-
rounded. Extraordinary efforts were then made
by the enemy to crush the centre and left ; rein-
forcements were brought from their right and
thrown upon the left of Negley and against Cruft,
Grose and Hazen. Negley, out of ammunition,
was compelled to almost cut his way out ; Grose's
and Cruft's Brigades of Palmer's Division, on
Negley's left, necessarily had to follow in his
wake, in a measure covering his retreat ; Hazen's
right, on Cruft's left, fell back and changed front
from southeast to northwest, pivoting on his left.
    To enable these troops to fall back, to afford
them protection, to gain time to execute the now
absolutely necessary movements in order to rec-
tify positions of troops and to form a new line
from Hazen's left toward the right, Rousseau's
Division was again ordered into the cedars. Gen-

eral Thomas himself gave the orders for the advance of the Regular Brigade, saying to its commander : " Shepherd, take your brigade in there," pointing southwest toward the cedar forest, "and stop the rebels." The brigade, without the battery, for which there was no suitable position in this movement, was at once put in march, advancing to the front (south) along the railroad and turnpike. After reaching the further side (south) of the open ground, it was suddenly directed to the right to enter the cedar forest, and after a change of direction slightly to the right, it was halted along the edge of the cedars facing southwest and west. During this movement the 2d Battalion of the 18th executed a change of front to the south, by companies on its left company, as if at ordinary battalion drill, then marched by the right flank into the cedars ; the other battalions moved up by their flanks and shortest routes, preserving proper intervals. This, all accounts agree, was about noon. The line was then advanced about fifty yards, until our retreating troops were in sight. The 15th held the right ; the 2d Battalion of the 18th the left, which rested less than one hundred yards from the south end of the woods ; each battalion occupied the best position the rocky ground in its front afforded, and the brigade covered a front of a little over one-fourth of a mile. Let us review the situation : Negley and Grose were retiring ; Cruft was covering Negley's retreat and following him ; Hazen's right was falling back ; the enemy's force was victorious and reinforced by three brigades—according to a Murfreesboro' rebel paper and Bragg's report—which were fresh and intact and commanded by Jackson, Preston and Adams, and in this breach stood the forlorn hope of the army, the Regular Brigade. Hazen's right retiring, left the left flank of the brigade uncovered, but John Beatty's Brigade covered that point and the rear in reserve ; on the right of the brigade, Scribner came up to cover that flank and to connect with troops still further on the right. As soon as the front of a battalion was clear of our retiring troops, its fire commenced ; this waiting for our men to retire, and, meanwhile, receiving the enemy's fire without being able to reply, was the most trying time of all. The firing commenced at the left as soon as Cruft's men—so reported by a staff officer—had withdrawn, and soon rose into a continuous roar. Capt. Oscar A. Mack, on General Thomas' staff, who approached the brigade with orders, and was severely wounded, declared the din of the fire to have been appalling. The first line of the enemy were scattered like chaff; their second line brought to a halt and held. The report of the men, especially, is that there was a third line, which coming up, fixed bayonets and with the remnants of the other two lines prepared for a charge. General Negley, with some of his men, united with the 15th, our right, and with them resisted the advance of his pursuers. Part of Scribner's Brigade formed on Negley's right; John Beatty covered the left and rear of the brigade. Officers and men were falling all along the line, but not a man turned his back to the enemy; every one stood up to his work and strove to be worthy of the hope placed in him, and to do credit to the Regular Brigade. General Thomas' orders had been obeyed; the enemy's onslaught on the centre had been repulsed, and his victorious troops brought to a halt; the rebels had been stopped, and the key of the battlefield secured, but at a loss of nearly half of the infantry force of the brigade. The new lines along the turnpike and railroad having been formed, troops moved into position, artillery posted to protect and cover the new lines, the right of the brigade received orders to fall back; the movement was executed under the protection of the battery, but unmolested by the enemy, from right to left in perfect order, one battalion moving after the other by the right of companies through the cedars to the rear. Lieut. Ludlow's section of the battery had been detached to the front and right to cover the retreat of the right of the brigade. It was a bitter disappointment to obey orders then, but as the object of the advance of the brigade had been achieved, its further exposure would have been useless, and could only have resulted in its annihilation ; still, this was not understood at the time by the officers and men of the brigade. When the heads of companies debouched from the woods, they were exposed to a tornado of artillery fire from rebel batteries to our left. From the position of the brigade in the cedars to a short distance outside, it was a gentle decline, the ground then again commenced to rise as far as the pike and railroad ; about one hundred yards from the woods, on higher ground, the brigade reformed and faced the enemy ; as there was no pursuit, it fell back of our new lines and joined again its battery in proper supporting position. Here roll was called, reports were made, and now the loss of the brigade was fully understood. John Beatty's and Scribner's Brigades fell back with the left and right of the Regular Brigade, and the artillery opened on the woods as soon as the brigade was out of them.

When the action opened in the cedars, Major Slemmer, of the 16th, was badly wounded, and Capt. Crofton took command ; almost immediately after giving the command to retire, Major Carpenter fell, mortally wounded, struck by six bullets, and the command of the 19th devolved on Capt. Mulligan ; on the retreat between the cedars and the railroad, Major King, of the 15th, was disabled, and Capt. Fulmer assumed command ; in the cedars, in the 1st Battalion of the 18th, Capt. Kneass was killed and Lieut. McConnell mortally wounded; in the 2d Battalion of the 18th, Lieut. Hitchcock was killed and Lieut. Simons mortally wounded; in the 15th Capt. Wise was mortally wounded; Major Townsend had his horse shot under him; the Adjutant of the 1st Battalion of the 18th had his horse wounded; and the Adjutant of the 2d Battalion had his killed under him, When the brigade was again in its supporting position, its left wing was committed for the remainder of the battle to Major Townsend, the right wing, deprived of its field officers, needing more the attention of the Brigade Commander.

This closed the enemy's and our operations for that day as far as active participation by the Regular Brigade was concerned; the battery, however, continued to play on the enemy's position, and when later in the afternoon an attack was made to the left of the brigade, it assisted in the repulse of the enemy in that quarter. During the night parties were organized to collect the wounded of the brigade; the pickets of the enemy and of the brigade were within speaking distance, and one of the parties was captured; another party claimed to be an informal flag of truce, asking for the privilege to collect our wounded, and thus after some parleying was permitted to return. During the night also our lines were straightened out; positions changed; the

right of the first division of the left wing posted
on the left of the turnpike, by which movement
our front was thrown back about three hundred
yards ; and the left wing formed on a new line
toward Stone River; this gave us a shorter line,
more reserves, and allowed the Regular Brigade,
at about 4 o'clock A. M., of the 1st of January,
to fall back to a little piece of woods near General Rosecrans' headquarters, there to bivouac
and seek rest.

Early on the 1st of January, 1863, the brigade,
with its battery, was ordered to the right to support McCook's wing, against which demonstra-
tions were made, and several positions were held
by it without coming into action. Shortly after
two o'clock the brigade was ordered to Stewart's
Creek; having marched about four miles, it received orders to return double quick, and marched
nearly the whole distance at that gait. Night
coming on, the brigade bivouacked again to the
left of the pike, near General Rosecrans' headquarters.

On the morning of the 2d of January, before
breakfast, the brigade advanced under heavy artillery fire to the support of the left wing, remain-
ing as its support in different positions during the
day and night ; the battery, being in action off
and on during the day, assisted in the enemy's
repulse by the left wing in the afternoon of the
day.

On the morning of the 3d, the fourth day of the battle, the battery opened fire upon one of the enemy, which was annoying our troops, and soon silenced and drove it from its position. During the forenoon the brigade and battery advanced again to its position, the key of the field, held on the 31st of December, threw up slight intrenchments and held them for the remainder of the battle. The heavy rains during the day filled the ditches partly with water and rendered them almost untenable, while the surrounding ground was fast turning into a bed of mud ; the men, at their option, could stand or recline in water or mud, but not a word of discontent escaped their lips in this trying and painful, as well as arduous and dangerous service. About 6 p. m., under the cover of the brigade and other batteries, an attack was made to the front by parts of John Beatty's and Spear's Brigades ; this attack, though spreading to the front of the brigade, required on its part only increased watchfulness to prevent surprise in case of a reverse ; the battery, however, was actively engaged in shelling the enemy's position in the woods to our front, south.

Before daylight of the morning of the fourth, the brigade pickets reported the retreat of the enemy. The day, Sunday, was spent in the sad duty of collecting the dead of the brigade, who were interred at night by moonlight and with military honors just in front of the intrenchments.

2

Thus ended the battle of Stone River, or Murfreesboro'; and here it may be proper to relate a few of the many incidents occurring in and during it, showing the spirit which pervaded the officers and men of the brigade, ready to laugh one moment, the next to suffer, and, if need be, to die.

During the fight at noon of the 31st of Dec., the color-bearer of the 2d Battalion of the 18th was killed by a shot in the head and fell with and on the colors; the color-guard at once raised the flag, when the top became entangled in a low cedar; the Adjutant of the battalion, then still mounted, finally called Lieut. Bisbee to the aid of the color-guard and the colors were at last free again and thrown to the breeze; it was a moment of great anxiety to all near, for it was understood that there was to be no losing of the colors. When the left reformed after leaving the cedars, Major Townsend, when on the rise took the colors and rode along the new line for all to see that and where the stand was to be made. Capt. Douglass, of the 18th, described the rebel artillery fire in the open field, as if a blacksmith shop full of rotten iron was being thrown at the command. When the brigade was reformed near its battery, there was a large pile of knapsacks back of it, and many men rested against it from time to time; pretty soon a rebel battery commenced firing solid shot at it, making the knapsacks fly in all

directions, but doing no other harm. For a
while it was a pastime to watch the solid shot
coming through the air, and one ball was
especially noticed, going apparently straight toward a man crossing the large open field to the
rear, coming from the hospital probably ; the ball
seemed to strike in front of and close to the man,
ricochetted and passed over the man, who at the
same time made a profound obeisance ; to all ap-
pearances the ball would have decapitated him,
had the man been erect ; a shout of laughter,
seemingly from all parts of the field, at the ludi-
crousness of the scene, relieved the anxious feel-
ing of suspense. But what a closing and begin-
ning of a year was that ! A large number of
officers and men, in fact all, were without rations
on the 1st and 2d, and parched corn, horse and
mule steaks were in demand and appreciated ; the
double quick back from near Stewart's Creek was
doubly hard on empty stomachs ; at last, on the
evening of the 2d, some bacon, flour and coffee
were received and helped to tide the command
over the worst ; though the men were hungry,
they were in the best possible spirits. When on
the 2d the brigade advanced by the right of companies double quick to the front, one man, seeing
a solid shot rolling along very leisurely, put his
foot out to stop it ; the opposing forces did not
overcome each other, and, the shot being stronger,
the man found himself nicely tripped and rolling

along with the ball, much to his surprise, and, not
being injured, to the merriment of his comrades.
The Battalion Quartermasters, with the teamsters,
servants, cooks and sick, defended their trains
against the charges of rebel cavalry repeatedly,
repulsing the enemy every time, and saving and
preserving their trains.   Of the three rebel
brigades of Jackson, Preston and Adams, General
Bragg, the commander of their army, says : " How
gallantly they moved to their work, and how
much they suffered in the determined effort
to accomplish it, will best appear from the reports
of subordinate commanders, and the statement of
losses therewith."   This shows some of the work
done by the Regular Brigade, and later by its
battery repulsing the determined charge of these
troops on to the left of the line of battle. General
Thomas, when asked why he sent the brigade
into the cedars, a regular holocaust, replied that
it became a necessity to do so.

The casualties in the brigade were fearful, and
almost all were suffered at noon of, and all oc-
curred on, the 31st of December.

The following statement is taken from official sources, and shows the casualties in the brigade in detail:

	NUMBER ENGAGED.		NUMBER KILLED.		NUMBER WOUNDED.		NUMBER CAPTURED.		TOTAL LOSS.	
	Commissioned Officers.	Enlisted Men.	Commissioned Officers.	Enlisted Men.	Commissioned Officers.	Enlisted Men.	Commissioned Officers.	Enlisted Men.	Commissioned Officers.	Enlisted Men.
Field and Staff of Brigade.........	4	...	...	...	...	...	...	...	...	...
1st Battalion, 15th U. S. Infantry...	16	304	2	10	3	74	...	17	5	101
1st " 16th "	15	293	...	16	7	127	...	16	7	159
1st " 19th "	10	198	1	6	6	55	...	7	1	68
1st " 18th "	16	273	1	27	6	109	...	2	7	138
2d " 18th "	16	298	1	30	5	98	...	5	6	133
Battery H, 5th Artillery.....	3	120	...	...	...	5	...	...	...	5
Total.... 80	80	1486	5	89	21	468	...	47	26	604
Aggregating.........	1566		94		489		47		630	

In his official report, General Rosecrans gives his loss as follows : Killed, 92 officers, 1,441 enlisted men ; total, 1,523 ; wounded, 384 officers, 6,861 enlisted men ; total, 7,245.

Total killed and wounded, 8,778 officers and men, or 20.22 % of the entire force in action ; the loss of prisoners, he states, will fall short of 2,800 officers and men.

The loss of the brigade compared with the loss of the army is as follows : Officers killed in the army, 92 ; in the brigade, 5 ; =5.4 % of army loss. Officers wounded in the army, 384 ; in the brigade, 21 ; =5.4 % of army loss. Enlisted men killed in the army, 1,441; in the brigade, 89 ; =6.1 % of army loss. Enlisted men wounded in the army, 6,861; in the brigade, 468 ; =6.8 % of army loss. Captured and missing in the army, 2,800 ; in the brigade, 47 ; =1.6 % of army loss.

The loss of the army in killed and wounded was about 20 % of the force in action ; the loss of the brigade in killed and wounded was 37 % of its strength in action.

The effective force of the army in the battle was, all told, 43,400 officers and men ; the effective force of the brigade taken into action was, all told, 1,566 officers and men, or 3.6 % of the strength of the army ; while the loss of killed and wounded of the brigade is 6.6 % of that of the army.

The loss of killed and wounded in Scribner's Brigade was reported as 208 officers and men, or

about 2.3 ⊄ of army loss ; in John Beatty's Brigade
as 281 officers and enlisted men, or about 3.2 ⊄ of
army loss ; while the three brigades were virtually
the same in strength of effective force.

Only two brigades in the whole army report a
larger loss of killed and wounded than the Regular Brigade; both were about 200 men stronger
than that brigade, and suffered losses before and
after the 31st December, while the loss of the
Regulars was all on that day ; the brigades were
Carlin's, of the right wing, loss 627—but lost on
the 30th 175 men, and a few more after the 31st ;
Grose's, of the left wing, 585—but lost before the
31st 10 men, and on the 2d of January, the brigade report states, met with a severe loss, not as
large as on the 31st, however.

These figures tell the tale, and it is doubtful if
in any other engagement of the war any organization under similar circumstances suffered as large
a loss.

The total number of men received by the general Government in its armies during the war, for
various periods, was 2,859,132 ; these, reduced to
a three years' standard, would make 2,320,272
men.

The average effective number of each 1,000
men in service has been computed at 693 men ;
this, applied to the number of men of the three
years' standard, would, in round numbers, give an
effective force of 1,608,000 men.

The total losses of the war, as near as it can be done with incomplete returns, has been computed to be : Killed in action, 44,238, or about 1.9 % of the effective force ; wounded in action, 280,000, or about 12 % of the effective force ; while the Regular Brigade lost on the 31st of December alone : Killed in action, 94, or 6 % of its effective strength ; wounded in action, 489, or 31 % of its effective strength. Of course, the above computations can be applied only in a general way, inasmuch as after 1861 the actual number of men in the United States service, on an average, was, in round numbers, only about 850,000 per year.

In his report of the battle, General Geo. H. Thomas says: " In the execution of this last movement, the Regular Brigade came under a most murderous fire * * * but with the co-operation of Scribner's and Beatty's Brigades and Guenther's and Loomis' Batteries, gallantly held its ground against overwhelming odds."

General Rousseau, in his report, speaks of the brigade as follows: " On that body of brave men the shock of battle fell heaviest, and its loss was most severe. Over one-third of the command fell, killed or wounded. But it stood up to the work and bravely breasted the storm, and, though Major King, commanding the 15th, and Major Slemmer (old Pickens), of the 16th, fell severely wounded, and Major Carpenter, commanding the 19th, fell dead in the last charge, together with

many officers and men, the brigade did not falter
for a moment. These three battalions were a
part of my old 4th Brigade at the battle of Shiloh. The 18th Infantry, Majors Townsend and
Caldwell commanding, were new troops to me,
but I am proud now to say we know each other.
* * * The brigade was admirably and gallantly
handled by Lieut.-Col. Shepherd. * * * Of the
batteries of Guenther and * * * I cannot say too
much. * * *· Without them we could not have
held our position in the centre."

Surgeon Eben Swift, Medical Director, De-
partment of the Cumberland, reports : "Much of
the heaviest loss sustained to-day fell upon our
Regular Battalions, brigaded under command of
Lieutenant-Colonel O. L. Shepherd, in holding
the cedar brake on the right of the centre against
the columns of the enemy sweeping down upon
them after having forced back our entire right
wing."

W. D. Bickham, who was on the field himself,
in his book, " Rosecrans' Campaign with the
Army of the Cumberland," published in March,
1863, makes the following record : "The Regular Brigade, Lieut.-Col. Shepherd at the head of
the column, moved steadily into the thickets, and
formed with Colonel John Beatty's Brigade on
the left, and Scribner's in close support. Directly
a dropping fire, like the big drops which precede
a storm, indicated the proximity of the enemy.

* * * But the enemy pushed hard. The gallant regulars resisted with the staunchness of their professional *esprit*, and refused to yield an inch. * * * The file firing of the regulars at this point was fearfully destructive."

"Pont Mercy," a correspondent of the New York *Tribune*, wrote from the battle-field : "There is a record, however, which shall be more amply made, when the Biography of the gallant Regular Brigade is ready for history. * * * Almost one-half the casualties were regulars, while they numbered less than one-fourth of the entire division. The missing indicates discipline and skill of officers with unmistakable emphasis. It was so in the sanguinary battle of Gaines' Mills on the Peninsula."

The Regular Brigade of the West had indeed sent greeting to their comrades in the East.

As already stated, the dead of the brigade were buried in front of the position held by it nearly throughout the battle ; the intention was to erect a monument over their remains, and officers and men subscribing liberally, a large sum was collected —about $4,000. The dead heroes rest now at the same point in the National Cemetery, established by the General Government ; and on the 12th of May, 1883, a monument made by the sculptor, Launt Thompson, was erected over their resting-place.

The foregoing is not a fancy painted history

of the brigade in this battle; it is not em-
bellished with rhetorical allusions to fire and
smoke, shot and shell, grape and canister, the
roar of the cannon, the rattling of the musketry,
the groans of the dying and wounded; it is a
simple and plain statement of facts in unembel-
lished terms; although the groans of the wounded
and dying, the rattling of the musketry, the roar
of the cannon, grape and canister, shot and shell,
and fire and smoke were constant accompani-
ments of the shifting scenes of this bloody and
destructive drama of the history of our country.

ROSTER

BRIGADE STAFF.

Lieutenant-Colonel O. L. Shepherd, 18th Infantry, Commanding Brigade.[5]

Captain N. C. Kinney, 18th Infantry, Quartermaster.[6]

1st Lieutenant Anson Mills, 18th Infantry, Commissary of Subsistence.[7]

1st Lieutenant Robert Sutherland, 18th Infantry Act'g Assist. Adjut.-Gen'l.[6]

1st BATTALION, 15th U. S. INFANTRY.

Major John H. King, Commanding Battalion.[3, 5]

1st Lieutenant F. D. Ogilby,[4] Adjutant.

Captain Jesse Fulmer.[6]

Captain W. W. Wise.[1]

Captain J. Bowman Bell.[1]

Captain Henry Keteltas.[6]

Captain Joseph S. Yorke.[3, 6]

1st Lieutenant Horace Jewett.[7]

1st Lieutenant Charles Wickoff.[7]

1st Lieutenant Sol. E. Woodward.[6]

1st Lieutenant W. B. Occlestone.[3, 4]

1st Lieutenant R. P. King.[6]

1st Lieutenant James Y. Semple.[4]

2d Lieutenant William Galloway.[6]

2d Lieutenant Roman H. Gray.[4]

The Regular Brigade.

1st Battalion, 16th U. S. Infantry.

Major A. J. Slemmer, Commanding.[3,4]
1st Lieutenant John Power, Adjutant.[3,6]
Captain R. E. A. Crofton.[7]
Captain R. P. Barry.[3,6]
Captain James Biddle.[6]
Captain N. L. Dykeman.[3,6]
Captain J. C. King.[3,6]
1st Lieutenant A. W. Alleyn.[6]
1st Lieutenant E. McConnell.[6]
1st Lieutenant W. H. Bartholomew.[3,4]
1st Lieutenant W. W. Arnold.[6]
1st Lieutenant J. C. Howland.[3,6]
1st Lieutenant R. E. Kellogg.[7]
2d Lieutenant S. E. St. Onge.[6]
2d Lieutenant W. J. Wedemeyer.[7]

1st Battalion, 18th U. S. Infantry.

Major J. N. Caldwell, Commanding.[5]
1st Lieutenant R. L. Morris, Adjutant.[4]
1st Lieutenant Dan'l W. Benham, Quartermaster.[7]
Captain Henry Douglass.[3,7]
Captain William S. Thurston.[6]
Captain David L. Wood.[3,6]
Captain Charles L. Kneass.[1]
Captain Robert B. Hull.[3,6]
Captain William H. H. Taylor.[6]
1st Lieutenant Joseph L. Proctor.[6]
1st Lieutenant Thomas T. Brand.[5]
1st Lieutenant Samuel I. Dick.[4]
1st Lieutenant Joseph McConnell.[2]
1st Lieutenant Gilbert S. Carpenter.[3,7]
2d Lieutenant Merrill N. Hutchinson.[5]
2d Lieutenant Ebenezer D. Harding.[6]
2d Lieutenant John J. Adair.[3,6]

2d Battalion, 18th U. S. Infantry.

Major Frederick Townsend, Commanding.[6]
1st Lieutenant Frederick Phisterer, Adjutant.[6]
1st Lieutenant Wm. P. McClery, Quartermaster.[6]
Captain Henry R. Mizner.[7]
Captain Charles E. Denison.[2]
Captain Henry Belknap.[6]
Captain Ai B. Thompson.[3, 5]
Captain Wm. J. Fetterman.[4]
Captain Henry Haymond.[3, 6]
Captain Ansel B. Denton.[6]
1st Lieutenant Morgan L. Ogden.[3, 6]
1st Lieutenant Herman G. Radcliff.[4]
1st Lieutenant James Simons.[2]
1st Lieutenant Henry B. Freeman.[7]
2d Lieutenant William H. Bisbee.[7]
2d Lieutenant John F. Hitchcock.[1]
2d Lieutenant Wilbur F. Arnold.[4]

1st Battalion, 19th U. S. Infantry.

Major S. D. Carpenter, Commanding.[1]
1st Lieutenant Howard E. Stansbury, Adjutant.[6]
Captain James B. Mulligan.[6]
1st Lieutenant A. H. Andrews.[6]
1st Lieutenant Jacob D. Jones.[6]
2d Lieutenant Joseph J. Waggoner.[4]
2d Lieutenant Wm. R. Lowe.[6]
2d Lieutenant Alfred Curtis.[6]
2d Lieutenant Chas. F. Miller.[4]
2d Lieutenant Geo. W. Johnson.[6]
2d Lieutenant Arthur B. Carpenter.[6]

Battery H, 5th U. S. Artillery.

1st Lieutenant F. L. Guenther, Commanding.[7]
2d Lieutenant Israel Ludlow.[6]
2d Lieutenant J. A. Fessenden.[7]

MEDICAL DEPARTMENT.

Assistant Surgeon Webster Lindsley, Acting Brigade Surgeon.[4]

Acting Assistant Surgeon Patton.[6]

Acting Assistant Surgeon Henderson.[6]

NOTES.

1 killed in battle of Stone River; 2 died of wounds received at Stone River.

3 wounded at Stone River; 4 died in service since Stone River.

5 retired; 6 resigned, discharged, mustered out, and out of service.

7 still in the U. S. Army, active list.

BATTLES AND ENGAGEMENTS

PARTICIPATED IN BY

THE REGULAR BRIGADE.

Stone River or Murfreesboro', Tenn., Dec. 31, 1862 to Jan. 3, 1863.

Eagleville, Tennessee, March 2, 1863.

Hover's Gap, Tennessee, June 26, 1863.

Chicamauga, Ga., September 19 to 21, 1863.

Mission Ridge, Tenn., November 25, 1863.

Buzzard Roost and Tunhill, Ga., Feb. 25 to 27, 1864.

Rocky Faced Ridge, Ga., May 5 to 9, 1864.

Resaca, Ga., May 13 to 15, 1864.

New Hope Church, Ga., May 28, June 1 and 4, 1864.

Kenesaw Mountain, Ga., June 22 and 30, 1864.

Neal Dow Station, Ga., July 3 and 4, 1864.

Peachtree Creek, Ga., July 20, 1864.

Atlanta, Ga., July 27 and 31, and August, 1864.

Utoy Creek, Ga., Aug. 7, 1864.

Jonesboro', Ga., September 1, 1864.

ENGAGEMENTS AND BATTLES PARTICIPATED IN
BY THE BATTALIONS BEFORE ORGANIZATION
OF THE REGULAR BRIGADE.

15th, 16th and 19th U. S. INFANTRY.

Shiloh, Tenn., April 7, 1862.
Corinth, Miss., May, 1862.

1st and 2d BATTALIONS, 18th U. S. INFANTRY.

Lick Creek, Miss., April 26, 1862.
Corinth, Miss., May, 1862.
Springfield to Texas, Ky., October 6, 1862.
Perryville or Chaplin Hill, Ky., October 8, 1862.